299
Short
Jokes for Kids

I.P. Grinning
&
I.P. Factly

DEDICATION

To Jacob & Riley.

What did the cop slug say to the escaping robber slug?

I'll get you next slime!

What do you call a green monster that you can flick across a room?

The bogey-man!

What's the biggest moth in the world?

A mam-moth!

Doctor, doctor, I've been telling everyone I'm a spider!

That's a web of lies!

What's the difference between an alien and a cookie?

Have you ever tried dunking an alien in your milk?

Doctor, doctor, I've just swallowed a sheep!

How do you feel?

Baa-d, really baa-d!

What happened when Ray discovered an alien with a laser gun?

He became an ex-Ray!

What happened when the chicken decided to sleep under a car?

She woke oily the next morning!

What do you call a guard with 100 legs?

A sentrypede!

What's the best way to help starving monsters?

Give them a hand!

What do ghost's love to eat?

Boo! Berry pie!

What do giant squid like for dinner?

Fish and ships!

What do goblins do when they finish school?

Their gnomework!

What do gorillas wear in the kitchen?

Ape-rons!

Where do ghosts go on holiday?

The Dead Sea!

Where did the pit bull terrier sit at the movies?

Anywhere it wanted!

Where did the seaweed find a job in the paper?

In the kelp wanted section!

Where did the stegosaurus get its groceries?

At the dino-store!

Where did the tyrannosaurus' poop go?

The dino-sewer!

Where did the young cows go on a school trip?

The moo-seum!

When should you take a pit bull terrier for a walk?

Whenever it wants!

What do ghosts say to each other?

Do you believe in people?

When would it be unlucky to see a black cat?

If you were a mouse!

When's the best time to buy a bird?

When it's going cheep!

Doctor, doctor, I feel hot and I've got a headache!

You must have flu!

No, I caught the bus!

What happened to the man who crossed a cow with a drummer?

He got a moo-sician!

What dinosaurs were good at soccer?

Dino-scores!

What do you call an elephant that watches TV all day?

A tele-phant!

When do monsters only eat children?

When they are on a diet!

When do witches come out on Halloween?

When it's time to go to sweep!

What's the best way to talk to aliens?

From a long way away!

What do you call an elephant that owns a small local food shop?

A deli-phant!

What's the difference between a monster and some potatoes?

You should never try mashing an alien!

What's the difference between an elephant and a cherry?

Cherries grow in trees!

What's the difference between Indian and African elephants?

About 5,000 miles!

What do ghosts put on their Christmas dinner?

Grave-y!

What's the most musical part of a chicken?

The drumstick!

What's the best television to have at Halloween?

A big scream TV!

What happened to the man who crossed a cow with a goat?

He got a coat!

What's the best thing to become if you've got high hopes?

A spaceman!

What's the brightest fish in the sea?

A starfish!

What's the daftest thing you can see at night?

A fool moon!

What do ghosts in love say?

You are Boo!-tiful!

What's the difference between a musician and a dead body?

One composes and the other decomposes!

What was the greatest dog detective called?

Sherlock Bones!

Doctor, doctor, when I press my leg it hurts, when I press my head it hurts, when I press my arm it hurts – what's wrong with me?

You've a broken finger!

What's the difference between an elephant and a grape?

You can't catch an elephant in your mouth!

What's the difference between an elephant and an empty packet of chips?

You can't pop an elephant!

What's brown and dangerous?

Shark infested cola!

What's brown and friendly?

Dolphin infested cola!

What's brown, fizzy, and lives in Australia?

Coca Koala!

What do ghouls like to eat for lunch?

Beans on ghost!

What was the farmer doing on the other side of the road?

He was catching all the chickens!

What was the most explosive of all the dinosaurs?

Dino-mites!

What was the name of the canary that flew into the pastry dish?

Tweetie Pie!

What happened to the man who crossed a cow with a wolf?

He got an animal that mooed at the full moon!

What was the saddest dinosaur?

Cry-ceratops!

What was the snail doing on the highway?

About one mile a week!

What was the tidiest dinosaur?

A cleaner-saurus!

What whale has the longest tongue in the animal kingdom?

Moby Lick!

Doctor, doctor, I think I'm a camera!

Hold it there - I'll be with you in a flash!

What would you get if you crossed a UFO with a wizard?

A flying sorcerer!

What do ghouls send to friends while on vacation?

Ghostcards!

What do you call a man who cuts grass?

Moe!

What do you call an elephant that tripped over?

A fell-ephant!

What size meals do glow worms prefer?

Light meals!

What snake might you use when driving?

A windshield viper!

What steps should you take if you a lion is charging towards you?

Big ones!

What meals do math teachers enjoy?

Square meals!

What steps should you take if you see an alien?

Large ones!

Doctor, doctor, my wife thinks she's a cat!

How can I help?

Can you stop her using the litter box?

What happened to the man who crossed a crab with a dinosaur?

He got a nip-lodocus!

What meteorites get their sums wrong at school?

Meteo-wrongs!

What might you call a clever duck?

A wise quacker!

What monster is 100 meters long, lives in Scotland, and never tidies its room?

The Loch Mess Monster!

What do you call an elephant in a mini?

Anything you like - it's not getting out in a hurry!

What monster is always playing tricks?

Prank-enstein!

What monster never gets wet?

Skeletons – they are always bone dry!

What monster visited the three bears?

Ghoul-dilocks!

What moves oxygen around zombie blood?

Dead blood cells!

What dinosaur often appeared at rodeos?

Bucking bronco-saurus!

What sort of band do vampires play in?

A blood group!

What do you call fossils that stay in river beds all day?

Lazy bones!

What kind of fast food do bees like?

Humburgers!

Doctor, doctor, my daughter thinks she's a hen!

Don't worry I can cure her!

What! And lose all the eggs?

What kind of fish like balloons?

Blowfish!

What kind of flour do zombies use to make bread?

Self-raising!

What kind of mad insect lives on the moon?

A luna-tic!

What happened to the man who crossed a dinosaur with a bluebottle?

He got a fly-ceratops!

What kind of math do owls like?

Owlgebra!

What is the naughtiest bird?

A mockingbird!

Doctor, doctor, I'm addicted to stealing chairs!

Please, do take a seat!

What kind of monsters are the quickest at eating humans?

Goblins!

What is the problem with twin witches?

You never know which witch is which!

What is the saddest bird in the world?

A bluebird!

What is the saddest creature in the ocean?

The blue whale!

What is the world's best jumper?

A hiccupping frog!

What is worse than finding a worm in your apple?

Finding half a worm!

What item from the bakery do young dogs love?

Pup-cakes!

What kind of alien spaceship gets upset easily?

A crying saucer!

What kind of ant is good at maths?

An account-ant!

What is green and pecks on trees?

Woody Wood Pickle!

What happened to the man who crossed a dinosaur with a leg?

He got a thigh-ceratops!

What do you call an ostrich at the South Pole?

Lost!

What is hairy with five legs and can disappear into a cloud?

A monster jumping out of a plane!

What is large and gray and gray and gray and gray and gray?

An elephant stuck in a revolving door!

What is noisier than your neighbor's dog barking?

Four of your neighbor's dogs barking!

What is purple with red spots, 20 legs, huge fangs, and has green goo oozing from its mouth?

I don't know but it's in your hair!

What is small, cuddly and highly dangerous?

A koala with a rocket launcher!

Doctor, doctor, I think I'm going to die!

No... that's the last thing you'll do!

What is special about the Mississippi river?

It has four eyes but can't see a thing!

What is tasty and lives in trees?

A meringue-utan!

What is black, white and red all over?

An embarrassed zebra!

What is a sheep's favorite animal at the zoo?

Baa-boon!

What is a snake's favorite dance?

The mamba!

What do you call a man with a car on his head?

Jack!

What is a snake's favorite subject at school?

Hiss-tory!

Doctor, doctor, I've just eaten 25 pancakes, or was it 26?

No, it was 27 pancakes... Stop this waffling!

What is a space alien's favorite thing to have on toast?

Baked beings!

Teacher: What are you going to be when you leave school?

Pupil: Old!

What happened to the man who crossed a dinosaur with a snack?

He got a chip-lodocus!

What is a vampire's favorite dog?

A bloodhound!

What is a vampire's favorite sport?

Bat-minton!

What is a young dog's favorite pizza topping?

Pup-peroni!

What is a cow's favorite party game?

Moo-sical chairs!

What has 6 legs, sucks blood, and talks in code?

A morse-quito!

What has antlers and sucks blood?

A moose-quito!

What has four wheels and flies?

A trash can!

What insect is good for your health?

Vitamin bee!

What is a baby bee?

A little humbug!

What do you call a man with a rabbit down his trousers?

Warren

What do you call an ant with frog's legs?

An ant-phibian!

Doctor, doctor, I've got wind! What can you give me for it?

Here's a kite!

What is a cat's favorite car?

Cat-illac!

What is a cat's favorite color?

Purrr-ple!

What happened to the man that crossed a plane with a dog?

He found himself a jet setter!

Teacher: What would I have if I had 2 melons in this hand and 6 bananas in the other hand?

Pupil: Big hands!

What happens if you cross a bear with a skunk?

You get Winnie the Pooheeey!

What happens if you cross the Queen of England with a brilliant caster of spells?

Someone very, very witch!

What happens if you train a two ton alien to walk on a lead?

You'll need to scoop some big poops!

What happened when the police said they were looking for a monster with one eye called Cyclops!

Everyone wanted to know what the other eye was called!

Doctor, doctor, I think I'm a cat!

How long have you thought that?

Ever since I was a kitten!

What happened when dinosaurs took buses?

They had to bring them back!

What does a cat call a peregrine falcon?

Fast food!

What happened when the boy announced he could lift an alien with both hands tied?

They couldn't find an alien that was tied up!

Teacher: What is the shortest month?

Pupil: May - with only three letters!

Teacher: How did Noah manage to design an ark?

Pupil: He was an ark-itect!

What happened when the cannibal was an hour late for lunch?

She was given the cold shoulder!

Teacher: What would you have if you took home three dogs today and five tomorrow?

Pupil: A very angry mom!

What happened to the man who crossed his dog with a tiger?

He had fewer friends visiting!

History teacher: Why is England so wet?

Pupil: Because Kings and Queens have reigned there for centuries!

What happened to the man that put a big fish into the plug socket?

He got an electric shark!

Doctor, doctor, I've got multiple personality disorderly!

Well get yourselves some more chairs and sit down!

History teacher: Why did the dinosaurs go extinct?

Pupil: I don't know, that's more your era than mine!

What happened to the man who cooked a dinosaur in pastry?

He got a pie-ceratops!

What happened to the man who crossed a new born snake with a trampoline?

He got a bouncing baby boa!

Doctor, doctor, I can't stop pulling horrible faces!

Why's that a problem?

Well, the people with the ugly faces don't like it!

What do you press on a keyboard to launch a rocket?

The spacebar!

What do you say when you greet an alien with four heads?

Hello, hello, hello, hello!

What do young dogs buy at the movies?

Pup-corn!

What do young ghosts hug at bedtime?

Deady bears!

Doctor, doctor, how long can you live without a brain?

I'm not sure, how old are you?

What do you call a woodpecker with no beak?

A headbanger!

What do you say to a thirsty tyrannosaur?

Tea, Rex?

What do clouds wear under their dresses?

Thunder pants!

What does a confused hen lay?

Scrambled eggs!

What does a queen do when she burps?

Issues a royal pardon!

What dogs make the best hairdressers?

Shampoodles!

Which dogs rip the mail every morning?

Tear-riers!

What drink don't spacemen have in outer space?

Gravi-tea!

What can aliens do that humans can't?

Count to 100 on their toes!

Doctor, doctor, I think I'm a pot of coffee!

I'll be with you in an instant!

What famous commander invented fireplaces?

Alexander the grate!

What fish do pirates use?

Swordfish!

What do you get when you cross a cow with a trampoline?

A milkshake!

What do you get if you cross a cow, a camel, and a trampoline?

Lumpy milkshakes!

What do you get if you cross a duck with a firework?

A firequaker!

What do you get if you cross a fridge and an ipod?

Cool music!

History teacher: Who was the biggest knight at King Arthur's round table?

Pupil: Sir Cumference!

What do you get if you cross a jellyfish and an aircraft?

A jellycopter!

What do you get if you cross a kangaroo and an elephant?

Big holes all over Australia!

What do you get if you cross a parrot with a pig?

A bird that hogs the conversation!

Doctor, doctor, how can I stop my nose running?

Take away its shoes!

What do fish like playing at parties?

Bass the parcel!

What did the dog say to the cat prancing across its yard?

Nothing, dogs can't talk!

What do you get if you cross a poodle with a chicken?

A cockapoodledoo!

What do you get if you cross a shark with a parrot?

An animal that can talk your head off!

What do you get if you cross a snake and a pie?

A pie-thon!

What do haunted ships have?

Skeleton crews!

Doctor, doctor, a shark ate the whole left half of my body!

Don't worry you are all right now!

What do horses play when not in the field?

Stable tennis!

What do cats enjoy at breakfast?

Mice Krispies!

What did the alien wear in summer?

Three pairs of sunglasses - one for each head!

What do lady aliens with huge teeth do at human parties?

They look for edible bachelors!

What do mice love to play?

Hide and squeak!

What do monsters call skateboarders?

Meals on wheels!

What do nursing cats always carry?

First aid kit-tens!

What did the skeleton in the monster band play?

Trom-bone!

What did the skeleton order for lunch?

Spare ribs!

What did the snail on the turtle's shell say?

Weeeeee!

What did the snake say when the teacher asked him a question?

Don't asp me!

What did the spider say to the fly?

I'm getting married do you want to come to the webbing?

What did the squeaky-clean dog say to the bug?

Long time no flea!

What did the squid do when it left school?

Joined the army!

What do lions say before they go hunting?

Let us prey!

What did the super-fast alien say?

Take me to your speeder!

What did the triceratops play in the school band?

The horn!

What did the vampire say after having work done on his teeth?

Fang-tastic!

What did the wolf say to the other wolves at the end of October?

Happy Howwwwwlloween!

What did the woodworm say to the table?

It's been nice gnawing you!

What did the writer do first when he decided to write a book on elephants?

He bought a ladder!

What did the zoo-keeper get when the elephant sneezed?

Out of the way!

What do you call a prehistoric burglar's dog?

Doyouthinktheysaurus Rex!

What do you call a rabbit with fleas?

Bugs Bunny!

Mother: You got a terrible mark, why do you think your teacher likes you?

Son: All those kisses she wrote on my test!

What did the alien say to the messy garden?

Take me to your weeder!

Man: Waiter waiter, there is a wasp in my soup!

Waiter: Sorry sir, we're out of flies today!

What did the ape say when it missed the phone call?

Who-rang-utang!

What did the Atlantic Ocean say to the Arctic Ocean?

Nothing, oceans can't speak!

What did the bee say to a naughty bee?

Bee-hive yourself!

Where do aliens go for their holidays?

Earth – for their annual trip around the Sun!

Mother: How did you manage to get told off so many times today?

Son: I'm an early riser!

What did the bees from Canada say to their cousins in Florida?

Swarm here isn't it!

What bird will steal soap from the bath?

A robber duck!

What did the buffalo say to his child on the first day of school?

Bi-son!

What did the boa constrictor say to the mouse?

I've got a crush on you!

What did the boy say when the teacher asked - what do you see at planetariums?

Starfish!

What did the bus driver say to the toad?

Hop on!

What did the calculator say to the boy?

You can count on me!

What did the cat get after visiting the doctor?

A purr-scription!

What did the cow who barged the other cow say?

Moo-ve!

What did the dog get at dog school when it had to take six from nine?

Flea!

Doctor, doctor, I feel like a pack of cards!

I'll deal with you later!

Mother: Did you take a bath?

Son: Why have you lost one?

What did the dog say at dog school when asked to take six from six?

Nothing!

Math Teacher: If I lay one egg here, three over here and then two more here, how many eggs will there be?

Pupil: None! You can't lay eggs!

My friend broke his arm raking leaves!

He fell out of the tree!

My friend is annoying. He wants to be on TV!

I wish he was on TV so I could switch him off!

My friend is blind and he went sky diving!

He had a great time but his seeing-eye dog was terrified!

My friend joined the fire service and was sacked the same day!

He'd always said, "Fight fire with fire"!

On what day should you expect banshees to start screeching?

Moanday!

Man: Waiter waiter, there are two flies in my soup!

Waiter: Yes it's buy one get one free today!

Son: There's a man at the front door with a beard!

Father: Tell him I've already got one!

Teacher: "Can you name six large animals that live in Africa?"

Boy: "Five elephants and a giraffe!"

How do you know when there's an elephant under your bed?

Your nose squashes against the ceiling!

What animal do cats like to sleep on?

A caterpillows!

What animal has even more lives than a cat?

A toad - it is always croaking!

What animal is always coming back to life?

Frogs, they croak all the time!

How do vampires keep clean?

They use a bat tub!

What animal is striped and bouncy?

A tiger on a trampoline!

What apes always come back no matter how hard you throw them?

Baboon-erangs!

What are a vampire's favorite fruit?

Blood oranges!

What are caterpillars' worst enemies?

Dog-erpillars!

How do you start a firefly race?

Ready steady glow!

How do you know your dog's been chasing ducks?

He's down in the mouth!

How do you know your kitchen floor is dirty?

The slugs leave a trail saying "clean me!"

How do you make a buffalo stew?

Keep it waiting for an hour!

How do you make a cheese puff?

Chase it round the house!

How do you know if an elephant's been in your car?

Peanut shells on the seats!

How do you make a glow worm laugh?

Cut off his tail, he'll be de-lighted!

How do you make a purple monkey?

Cross a red monkey with a blue one!

How do you make a strawberry shake?

Tell it a scary story!

Geography teacher: Where are the Andes?

Pupil: At the end of my sleevies!

How do you make a tissue dance?

You got to put a little BOOGIE into it!

How do you raise a baby elephant?

With a forklift!

How do you save an injured insect?

Call an ant-bulance!

How do you make a witch itch?

Take away her 'W'!

How do you send messages in the forest?

Moss code!

How do apes open bananas?

They use mon-keys!

How do cows move about the galaxy?

Through the Milky Way!

How do dogs like their eggs?

Pooched!

How do male monsters know they've met their future wife?

It's always love at first fright!

How do pigs hack trees down?

With pork chops!

How do prawns and clams communicate?

With shell-phones!

How do rabbits go on vacation?

By hare-plane!

How do sealions send love letters?

Seal-ed with a kiss!

History teacher: How did Vikings communicate?

Pupil: Norse code!

How do shark dentists work?

Very carefully!

How do sheep sing?

Baa-dly!

Doctor, doctor, I've got wind! Can you give me something?

Doctor: Yes, here's a kite!

How do sheep swim across rivers?

Baa-ckstroke!

How do sheepdogs talk to sheep?

They baa-rk!

How do skeletons talk to their friends far away?

On the tele-bone!

How do snails get their shells so shiny?

They use snail varnish!

How do squids in love walk along the sea floor?

Arm in arm in arm in arm in arm in arm...

How do ghosts score in a game of soccer?

By kicking the ball in the ghouls!

How do the police scare bugs away?

They call for the S.W.A.T. team!

⁺ired zombies look?

.!

How do monkeys use stairs?

They slide down the banana-ster!

How can you tell if your mum keeps dinosaurs in the refrigerator?

The door won't shut!

How can you tell the difference between a suit and a dog?

A suit is jacket and pants but a dog just pants!

How can you tell which end of a worm is the head?

Tickle it in the middle and see which end laughs!

At what kind of market might a dog pick up something new?

A flea market!

Geography teacher: What did Delaware...?

Pupil: A New Jersey!

Headmaster: Why did you pass everything except history class?

Pupil: I didn't take history!

How did the baker know the vampire had broken in?

All the jelly doughnuts were empty!

How did a hideous alien persuade a pretty girl to kiss it?

With a stun gun!

How did Baron Frankenstein stop his monster biting his nails?

He put in screws instead!

How did Frankenstein's monster wake up?

Bolt upright!

ABOUT THE AUTHOR

IP Grinning is the happy father of 7 and 9 year old boys. Their hilariously awful attempts to make up their own jokes inspired the IP Grinning & IP Factly series of joke books for kids.

Hopefully you'll enjoy this book as much as he enjoyed writing it.

Lightning Source UK Ltd.
Milton Keynes UK
UKHW020705271218
334529UK00023B/1198/P